BOOZE BASICS

BOOZE BASICS

A COMPLETE GUIDE TO THE DOS AND DON'TS OF DRINKING

EMILY MILES

DOG 'n' BONE

This edition published in 2019 by Dog 'n' Bone Books
an imprint of Ryland Peters & Small Ltd
20–21 Jockey's Fields   341 E 116th St
London WC1R 4BW   New York, NY 10029

Previously published in 2014 as *How to Drink and Not Look
Like an Idiot.*

www.rylandpeters.com

10 9 8 7 6 5 4 3 2 1

Text © Emily Miles 2014
Design and illustration © Dog 'n' Bone Books 2014

A CIP catalog record for this book is available from the Library
of Congress and the British Library.

ISBN-13: 978 1 911026 94 5

Printed in China

Editors: Helen Ridge and Pete Jorgensen
Designer: Jerry Goldie
Illustration: John Riordan

CONTENTS

"When I read about the evils of drinking, I gave up reading."

HENRY YOUNGMAN

CHAPTER 1

INTRODUCTION:
ALL IN GOOD TASTE

Friday night at the local bar: revelers swig beer, slam shots, and repeat until failure. Happy hour turns into greasy food o'clock, then everyone staggers home, job done. Most of us have been there (and had fun doing it). But there comes a time when you want to graduate from downing cheap booze in sticky venues to something a little more sophisticated. And, as the flood of new artisan alcohols and serious bars that we're currently enjoying attest, refinement is enjoying a resurgence—which means there has never been a better time to know how to drink well.

THE JOURNEY BEGINS

Granted, developing the barroom presence of *Mad Men's* Don Draper will take practice, and yes, demonstrating the facility with alcohol of James Bond requires perseverance. You will have to venture a little farther down the wine list than "second least expensive"; you'll have to invest some time and some money into tasting spirits and buying bottles, and there will be quite a few martinis to drink—just to check that you definitely prefer an olive to a twist. (It's a tough job, etc.) But once you've decided that you want to know more, the following chapters will provide the tips, tricks, and tools to ensure you know what you're doing—whether you're in a high-end restaurant or navigating the menu in a downtown cocktail bar.

First, though, we need to understand why drinking well is so important—and how our drinking culture has evolved. The tongue-loosening, ice-breaking effects of alcohol have been lubricating the wheels of society for millennia. Ever since humankind emerged from the primordial soup, we have been squirreling things away into pots, kegs, barrels, and bottles in the hope that fermentation (when sugar plus yeast equals alcohol and CO_2) might occur.

It's universal: wherever you travel in the world, there will be a potent brew—usually based on the dominant staple crop in that area (rice, wheat, potato, etc.)—that a local will cheerfully pour down your throat. It marks births, as the baby's head is wetted, and death, as a glass is raised at a

No backpacker's trip to Peru is complete without trying the local spirit, pisco.

wake. It signifies spiritual rites, celebration, friendship, deals done, and relationships brokered. But for something so tightly woven into the fabric of life, alcohol has not always been the hero of the piece. Once in a while, it's been vilified, handed a civil citation or ASBO, and run out of town.

"In wine there is wisdom, in beer there is Freedom, in water there is bacteria."

BENJAMIN FRANKLIN

A BRIEF HISTORY OF BOOZE

Back in the days before Starbucks, the Western world was awash with beer. It was safe to drink when water wasn't potable, it was cheap and easy to brew, and it was much weaker than the European lagers we're used to today (just as well, or no one would have got any work done). Although spirits and wine were made, they had since Roman times been the preserve of religious leaders and the aristocracy. Once foreign trade routes opened up, however, the drinking culture shifted—especially in the countries that were pioneering international commerce. In Britain, for example, the Dutch arrived with a new-fangled spirit called genever, the precursor to what we know as gin. Brits took to it with characteristic enthusiasm, and by the seventeenth century were knocking back around two pints a week.

The government of the time commissioned William Hogarth—a renowned society artist—to produce the equivalent of a "drink responsibly" campaign. The first of his brilliant etchings, *Beer Street*, showed wholesome English ale as the drink of choice for a healthy and happy society (not, perhaps, the advice today's health bodies would issue). In the second etching, *Gin Lane*, the story is one of vice, moral

depravity, and mother's ruin (a baby is tossed aside in favor of another jarful of gin). But although government cautioned against insobriety, the British have never banned booze—in fact, in 1854, an attempt to restrict the sale of ale on Sundays resulted in widespread rioting.

While Brits battled for their beer rights, elsewhere temperance movements were calling time on drinking in an attempt to promote piety and propriety. The most influential and notorious of these alcohol bans was America's Volstead Act, brought into force in 1919. Today, the mention of Prohibition brings to mind chiaroscuro images of trilby-wearing bootleggers, riotous speakeasies, and teapots filled with moonshine—but the reality was more dangerous. Racketeers and gangsters, such as Al Capone, would run a town's black-market trade, cutting any decent alcohol with water and rough grain spirit to create hooch, or gut rot, as it was more accurately known. The best of it would get you sloshed, the worst was a ticket to the morgue.

The only way to stomach the bootleg liquor was by mixing it into cocktails, and, as necessity is the mother of invention, countless recipes were cooked up. While few endured post-Volstead, a handful—such as the Sidecar—made it into the classic cocktail canon. It may not have been molecular mixology, but the punters weren't complaining. In fact, ironically, it was Prohibition that ensured the cocktail's future, because those bartenders who were not prepared to work underground packed up their Boston shakers and headed to Europe.

Still reeling from the First World War, Europe was ready for a drink. The finest hotels in London, Paris, Vienna, and Rome opened so-called American bars to showcase this revolutionary style of drinking. One of the most pioneering of the bartenders in the exodus was a man named Harry

Craddock; his arrival at The Savoy on the Strand in London was serendipity, and the groundbreaking book of cocktails he created there remains in print today. It was the roaring Twenties, and enthusiastic Charleston dancers were fueled by martinis, Manhattans, and daiquiris. Drinks got shorter—as did the hemlines—and London was at the center of a social whirl. Liquor-starved Americans could jump on the new airliners and zip across the pond to imbibe alongside their (increasingly less) stiff-upper-lipped cousins.

This was the golden age of the cocktail—the drinks forged in its heat remain fundamental to any menu (if they're not on the cocktail list in the joint you're drinking in, it's time to move on and find a proper American Bar). But not only were the recipes of the Twenties legendary, so, too, were the drinkers.

Once prohibition hit, many US bartenders made their way to Europe in search of work. This helped to raise the popularity of the cocktail in cities such as London and Paris.

Writers such as Ernest Hemingway and F. Scott Fitzgerald were possessed of dry wit liberally lubricated by dry martinis. When it comes to drinking well, we have much to learn from them, and so their various wisdom has been quoted throughout this book.

WHEN GOOD DRINKS GO BAD

Every heyday must have its antithesis, and for the cocktail the end of the golden age can be summed up in a word: disco. In the Seventies, as dance floors lit up and fashion became more flammable, something terrible happened to what we

White suits and bright cocktails; never a good mix whilst attempting your best John Travolta impression on a crowded dancefloor.

were drinking. The pared-down recipes of the first half of the century were ditched in favor of alarming amounts of blue curaçao, swizzle sticks, umbrellas, and fruit salad. With the arrival of drinks such as the Harvey Wallbanger, the pina colada, and the tequila sunrise, it was clear that style had become more important than substance. These drinks were the gold lamé bell-bottoms of the bartender's art: fun to look at, but distinctly questionable when it came to taste. Wine brands began to appear—sickly mass-market concoctions, such as Blue Nun and Mateus Rosé, committing crimes against Bacchus (although at least there was a sense of democratization creeping into this hitherto elitist world).

In bars, flashiness and flair became ever more important. As Tom Cruise's bottle-flipping lothario Brian Flanagan disseminates in the movie *Cocktail*:

> *"The sex on the beach*
> *The schnapps made from peach*
> *The velvet hammer*
> *The Alabama slammer.*
> *I make things with juice and froth*
> *The pink squirrel*
> *The three-toed sloth."*

Froth and juice? Since when was that a proper drink? Where once a cocktail had showcased liquor in its coldest, purest form, there was now a clutch of "ritas" and "tinis" on menus, each fruitier than the last. A strawberry daiquiri had more in common with a Slush Puppie than a shot.

The base element of the cocktail—which should be a careful balance of bitter, sweet, and spirit—had been so bastardized that these drinks weren't about the kick of liquor any more. The aim wasn't even to disguise the taste of bad alcohol, but rather to make spirits accessible and easy to drink. The market was right for the arrival of alcopops. Critics argued that these were targeted at underage drinkers to wean them off soda pop—it was an easy case to make. But irrespective of who was drinking them, alcopops were a neat shorthand to show how far cocktails had been distanced from the bartender's craft. Hooch, Breezers, and WKD were the TV dinner of the drinks industry: flip off the lid, and serve. No anticipation, no sophistication—just consumption.

Fashions quickly evolve, however. Perhaps taking the lead from our changing relationship with food, we now care more about the provenance and production of alcohol than ever before. Winemakers talk increasingly about "terroir"—where the grapes are grown and the influence this has on the wine. The industry has been making crashing leaps forward in terms of the quality of production, especially at the more accessible end of the price spectrum, and bland brands are being usurped by interesting makers. Speakeasy-style bars are emerging, but rather than serving bootlegged spirits, they are preparing artisan-distilled products shaken and served as classic drinks. Bartenders worthy of Michelin stars are becoming international figures. In bars and pubs, craft beers are steadily replacing the mass-market pints. The new age of the conscious consumer is here, and we're demanding a better drink in our glass and a classier bar in which to drink it. Cheers to that.

CHAPTER 2

WINE:
YOUR PASS NOTES

GETTING TO GRIPS WITH GRAPES

Let's start with **chardonnay**, but before you announce yourself as a member of the ABC ("anything but chardonnay") hate group, consider that in past years this grape has been subjected to some pretty rough treatment by New World winemakers. While in cooler climates, it produces a dry, buttery, mineral-rich wine, under a hotter sun, with less delicate handling, its elegance can be obliterated by bucket-loads of oak (that sickly vanilla flavor, which is made even worse if served warm and in mugs at a house party).

The very best chardonnay in the world is made in Burgundy, France, and is called Chablis. Mâcon and Pouilly-Fuissé are the other French big hitters. Winemaking in the New World has become far more refined in recent years, and you can now get some incredible chardonnays from South Africa, New Zealand, Australia, and the US. But if you want to play it safe because you hate a lot of oakiness, then stick to European bottles.

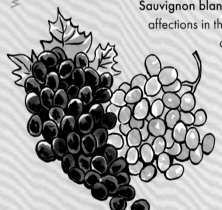

Sauvignon blanc muscled its way into our affections in the Nineties, as wine-bar and restaurant chains began to push it as an alternative to over-oaked chardonnays. It is characteristically crisp, dry, and super-refreshing. Taste- and aroma-wise, picture a Downton Abbey lawn party: scents of flowers, just-cut grass, herbs, nettles, and gooseberries. The headline-act "sav blancs" are Sancerre and Pouilly-Fumé, made in France's Loire Valley, but New Zealand's cool-climate Marlborough region produces some stellar examples, too, which have pungent flavors of tropical fruit.

Riesling, the unsung hero of the grape world, is often overlooked by (non-German-speaking) consumers because of its indecipherable labels. However, its aromatic wines are a great bet if you're looking for something to go with Thai or Pan-Asian food. Rieslings have intense tropical fruit and peachy flavors, and—as they age—smell a little like gasoline (this is not a tease, I promise). The best ones come from Germany, and have different quality classifications, starting with the fruity and off-dry Qualitätswein bestimmter Anbaugebiete category. Easy for you to say.

The diva of the grape world is **pinot noir**: high-maintenance and thin-skinned. But while it may be tricky to grow, thriving only in very specific regions of France, the cool climes of New Zealand, and in northern California and Oregon in the US, it is exceptionally easy to drink, producing delicate, fruity flavored (strawberry, raspberry, cherry) wines that can sometimes smell slightly agricultural, or even of leather. Pinot noir's fussiness means it is naturally scarce, and so the best of it is very expensive. The premium examples are from Burgundy in France—it'll say "Bourgogne" on the label. Avoid it if it appears to come from a very hot country, as the wine is likely to be jammy and flabby. Importantly, PN is one of the only three grapes that can be used to make Champagne—and for that alone we love it.

Forget Brangelina or the Clintons. **Cabernet sauvignon** and **merlot** are a real power couple. Individually, they are

OK—merlot is the paunchier half of the duo, rounded and a bit soft, while cab sav is acidic, full of tannin, and ages well—but together they are dynamite. When blended, these grapes make the most prestigious of all red wines, Claret, which is produced in Bordeaux, France. The celebrity Bordeaux regions include Saint-Emilion, Pomerol, Médoc, and Graves, and you'll pay top dollar for the privilege of drinking their wines. Flavor-wise, we're talking blackcurrant, berries, and tobacco and woody notes. With age, the wines become more complex, and the heavy tannins of youth mellow and soften to give depth and structure. These grapes are also widely used outside France. In Argentina, they are often combined with malbec to create excellent wines, while in California look out for those from the Napa Valley or Sonoma. In South Africa, it's all about the Western Cape wine region—Stellenbosch in particular.

Syrah is a slippery grape to pin down. Not only is it slightly schizophrenic, in that its southern hemisphere alter ego is known as **shiraz**, but it also varies wildly in terms of quality and characteristics. In cooler regions, syrah tends to make very dark wine, with flavors of blackberry and dark chocolate, while Aussie versions of shiraz are sweeter, more alcoholic, and fruitier, with soft tannins and mild acidity. For those used to more structured Old-World wines, shiraz from

"A classification is only important if it means something to consumers."
COUNT STEPHAN VON NEIPPERG,
OWNER OF SIX CELEBRATED
BORDEAUX WINE CELLARS

Oz can seem headache-inducingly intense. The most famous areas for the grape are in the Rhône, such as Côte-Rôtie, while, down under, celebrated brands such as Penfolds make dreamy shiraz in the Barossa Valley. Unfortunately for the wine-loving amateur, the regions that make the best shiraz are also responsible for the worst, so watch out for bottles with the origin label "South Eastern Australia," as this is often an indication of poor quality.

Because of its sensitivity to frost and disease, **malbec** fell out of favor in Bordeaux in the Fifties, so it set out to find fame and fortune in other climes. The streets of Mendoza, in Argentina, duly turned out to be paved with gold for the grape. With access to a little more sunshine and altitude, its robust tannins and juicy flavors came to the fore to create gutsy reds, which are fantastic with a succulent steak. (Handily, Argentina is pretty good at those, too.) Malbec represents excellent value on wine lists, and you are virtually guaranteed a full-bodied, almost violet-colored wine, with flavors of intense fruit.

CHAMPAGNE AND SPARKLING WINE

Napoleon Bonaparte famously said,

*"In victory you deserve Champagne.
In defeat you need it."*

On that basis, it's safe to assume that the French general got through quite a lot of the stuff. He had a fair point, though: no drink so strongly signifies our need to celebrate, commiserate, or indulge as Champagne. But is it really any better than any of the other sparkling wines available?

Well, in the same way that a LaFerrari sports car commands a few extra bucks because it's limited-edition, so, too, can Champagne charge a premium because it's naturally quantity-limited. There are only a handful of designated vineyards surrounding the cities of Reims and Epernay in France that may produce the coveted bubbles. And making it is a tricky business.

*"Come quickly,
I am drinking the stars."*

These are the words the Benedictine monk Dom Pérignon was heard to cry on discovering that bubbles had formed in his wine—or at least, that's how the myth goes. In reality, the Dom was one of the winemakers who dedicated themselves to trying to stop the secondary fermentation in wine, which is what caused the sparkle. Why? Because at that time, walking through a wine cellar in spring was a deadly business—iron face masks were mandatory—as up to 90 per cent of the stock exploded in the bottle.

In the late 1600s, Pérignon began to insist on using specific production methods and pinot noir grapes to try to improve the wine's quality and—ironically—reduce the chance of bubbles. But France was developing a taste for his lively wines. English glassblowers went to work to make bottles strong enough to withstand the CO_2 pressure, and an export market developed. In London, the Marquis St-Evremond convinced his circle of friends, known as Epicureans, that Champagne was the height of style. And its fame spread.

With only a 10 per cent chance of success, it's testament to the qualities of Champagne that early manufacturers were willing to persevere with the product.

Another Champagne celebrity, the Widow Clicquot (whose house, Veuve Clicquot, is still the most recognizable), spread the fame of Champagne to the czars of Russia, who adored her wines for two reasons: their lack of sediment and their sweetness. To understand both, we need to know how Champagne is made.

From grape to glass

Just a short train journey from Paris finds you among Champagne's patchwork of immaculately trained vines. There are three main varieties grown, two producing red grapes (pinot noir and pinot meunier) and one white, chardonnay. Didn't realize that red grapes can make white wine? Yep. The color is in the skin, not the juice, so as long as the skins are discarded, you'll get a white wine.

The chalk-covered hillsides, which were formed when the area used to be coastline, are split into different quality classifications, depending on the village they belong to. Grand Cru are the best, followed by Premier Cru, and, lastly, Deuxième Cru. Although there are around 20,000 owners of vineyards in the area, only 25 per cent of them actually make their own wine. The rest sell their valuable crop on to larger Champagne houses.

The first stage of Champagne-making is like that of any wine: the grapes are harvested and gently pressed, and the juices set aside to make a still base wine. The base wines are often blended with still wines from previous years, to ensure that the house style tastes consistent (these are "non-vintage" Champagnes). If it's a particularly good year, a vintage will be declared, and only the best wines from that particular harvest can go into the bottle. If you see a year on a bottle of

> *"I only drink Champagne when I'm happy and when I'm sad. Sometimes I drink it when I'm alone. When I have company I consider it obligatory. I trifle with it if I'm not in a hurry and drink it when I am, otherwise I never touch the stuff unless I am thirsty."*
>
> **LILY BOLLINGER**

Champagne, it's a signal that what's inside is of exceptionally high quality—it will have been aged for at least six years, and will have legs for much longer than that.

Once the base wine is blended, it's then mixed with a small amount of sugar and yeast, and bottled. This magic combination causes a second fermentation, meaning that the alcohol content in the wine creeps up, and that the by-product of CO_2 (carbon dioxide) can't escape from the bottle and so dissolves into the liquid. The Champagne is then left to mature in the cool chalk cellars, which were originally Roman quarries, and the yeast in the wine imparts a lovely toasty, biscuity character.

Next up, we see where Widow Clicquot's ingenuity comes into play. Once the yeast has done its job, it leaves behind a sediment that needs to be removed from the bottle. For this, Mrs. Clicquot invented the riddling rack, a medieval-sounding device that gradually tips the bottle upside down so the sediment collects in the neck. The neck of the bottle is frozen and the bottle uncapped. With that, the pressure of the bubbly wine pushes out the sediment ice cube, leaving behind a clean product.

The bottle then has to be topped up with a portion of wine

And now to the best bit: take a decent sip of wine and let it roll around your mouth. Channel the twin personalities of Hannibal Lecter and your favorite TV wine expert and try to suck in a little air—the slurping sound is perfectly acceptable, although drooling is not. This isn't purely to show off: the air will help you detect all the aromas in the wine. Making sure that you swill it all around your mouth is important, too, as different parts of your tongue are more sensitive to different characteristics: sweetness on the tip, and sourness at the back and sides, for example. Now swallow, and concentrate.

What to look for

You need to rate the wine across the following categories: sweetness, acidity, body, tannin levels, and flavor.

Sweetness is an easy one. First, we're used to detecting it, and second, the vast majority of wines are dry, so you should feel confident making a judgment. Acidity is really important. It's what makes wine literally mouth-watering, and it's needed to counteract sweetness in white wine. If a mouthful of Sauvignon Blanc really gets your juices going, then it's safe to say it has "good acidity." Body is a harder concept to nail, but if you think of it in terms of the viscosity of the liquid— for example, a really heavy Aussie Shiraz versus a light Beaujolais—then you'll be on the mark. Tannin may sound like one for the wine buffs, but as long as you have experienced a good cup of tea (hold the cream and sugar) or eaten a still-green banana, then you already know how to recognize that drying, astringent sensation. Tannin comes from the skin of the grape (also the part that gives wine its color), so, as a rule of thumb, darker wines have more tannin. In fine wine, it's the softening tannins that make it age well.

When you come to describe the flavor of the wine, the main thing to remember is that taste is subjective, so nothing that you think is wrong. Wine buffs use adjectives that may sound random, but they actually fall into a few groups: fruits, flowers, vegetables, and then the more unusual ones, such as leather, gasoline, and tobacco. The more wine you taste, the more flavors you'll be able to pick up on, and, as mentioned already, certain grapes tend to have certain flavors associated with them.

MATCHING WINE AND FOOD

Wine- and food-matching can be real alchemy—with a couple of tricks, you can take a bottle of basic wine and a pretty decent meal, then throw them together to create gastronomic gold. As a general rule, look to balance the richness of the dish with the heaviness of the wine: delicate fish dishes need lightweight wines; robust game flavors are best partnered by full-bodied reds. You'll soon find you do it instinctively.

If you're ever uncertain about which wine to choose, go for one that comes from the same region as your food— chances are, the locals have been developing their wines to complement the dishes they serve for decades. This is especially true of Italian food and wine. Its tomato-based dishes and Mediterranean flavors are often high in acidity. Consequently, they need wine that is high in acidity to match, or else the wines can taste dull and lifeless. Luckily, most Italian reds are laden with food-friendly acidity and so will perfectly partner your spaghetti alla puttanesca. In addition to the famous wines of Chianti, names to look out for are Barolo, Brunello, and Barbera. Bellissimo.

Another joyful food- and wine-matching partnership is the effect a mouth-watering steak can have on a tannin-laden red. That glass of cab sav, which you thought you had misordered because it seemed way too astringent, will transform the second you get meat involved. The protein in the steak reacts with the tannin in the wine and softens it, making your wine taste smoother, more refined, and more expensive than it may have been (the moral here is to ensure red wine is served only once the meal arrives). That same tannin-heavy wine, however, would be a disaster for someone who had ordered mackerel, as tannin with oily fish or salt can taste bitter and unpleasant. One to watch out for.

You already know that port and cheese are a classic combination. The reason they go together isn't just because the "pass to the left" crew had a penchant for Stilton, but rather because the sweetness of the fortified wine and the saltiness of the cheese enhance each other's flavors. Use this theory to match sweet pudding wines with pâté, for example, and people will be clamoring for an invitation to your next dinner party.

ORDERING WINE IN A RESTAURANT

It can be intimidating to arrive at a restaurant to find a waiter archly handing you a wine list that's thicker than Yellow Pages, and especially if it seems like it's written in Dothraki. The fundamental thing to remember is that—whatever your level of wine knowledge—you're the customer and whatever you say goes. The sommelier (identified by a small lapel pin depicting a bunch of grapes, and a nonchalant air of expertise) is your friend. A good one, and most of them are, isn't there to upsell you wine, but rather to help you pick something that will match your budget and the various dishes you're ordering. To become a Master Sommelier takes degree-level formal training and years of experience, and he (or she) will be keen to tell you as much as you want to know about the wines that he has curated for the restaurant's cellar. He will also have tasted the dishes on the menu, which is a head start on which bottles will make a good match.

If your budget is tight—or you simply need to make a speedy decision—then don't overlook the house wine. This isn't a cop-out option: a good restaurant will have dedicated plenty of time to searching out a red and a white that represent excellent value, and which they are happy to put their name to. In fact, if the house wine isn't decent, it's a pretty clear indication that this isn't an establishment that deserves your custom.

If you have the requisite wallet-width to look further down the list, then, to get the best value, avoid the obvious traps of the big-label French wines. Although they may be delicious, wines such as Chablis, Sancerre, and the famous Clarets will all come with a premium markup that can be avoided by venturing a little off-piste. (However, if you're ordering to impress clients, then go ahead!) Ask the sommelier for his favorite new discovery, which is unlikely to be an established—and therefore expensive—Château. Or, if you want a safe-bet red that won't break the bank, plump for a juicy Argentinian malbec. For whites, a French wine from the Languedoc called Picpoul de Pinet is currently popping up on a lot of lists, and is a reliable crowd-pleaser.

How to send a wine back

Restaurants aren't offering you a try-before-you-buy service when they ask if you would like to taste the wine. Rather, this is your chance to check that the wine is in good condition. (Unfortunately, if you don't like what you've ordered, there is little you can do, other than remember to avoid it next time.)

Once in a while you may come across a faulty bottle—wine is, after all, a natural product—and if you do, you're well within your rights to send it back. The most common fault people cite is "corked" wine. This doesn't mean that there are bits of cork floating in the liquid (that's just because someone inexperienced has pushed in the corkscrew too far). It's actually when wine has come into contact with a bad cork—one that's been gormandized by microorganisms—during its aging process, and which has corrupted the liquid. Around 7 per cent of bottles are affected. Corked wine will smell somewhere between a wet dog and a mildewed bathroom. If you think there's even a hint of murkiness, don't feel afraid to ask the sommelier for a second opinion.

Another fault to watch out for is oxidized wine, which is when air has crept into the bottle during aging. The wine will taste vinegary, and it may discolor, too, looking dull and brown. Heat is also an enemy of wine and can result in a cooked, or "maderized," bottle. Signs to watch out for are a cork that doesn't sit flush with the bottle (it may have been pushed out when warm wine has expanded), or a jammy sweetness in what should be a dry wine.

If in doubt, talk to the sommelier. Even if he disagrees with your opinion, he's unlikely to argue in the restaurant. Instead, he'll switch the bottle and, if he has any sense, polish off the rejected wine once he's clocked out. Everyone's a winner.

MAKING CHEAP WINE TASTE BETTER

To start with, exercise a little expectation management—no one is going to be convinced you've uncorked a vintage Bordeaux worth hundreds when you've actually unscrewed a hugely inferior wine, but you can really significantly improve the taste of your wine by using the right glasses to serve it in. You will need to look on this as a long-term investment—we're talking about $50 (£30) a glass, so you might want to leave your clumsier friends off the guest list—but it will pay off every time you open a bottle. Brands that carry a lead crystal sommelier range are an excellent place to start. Glasses from manufacturers such as Riedel, Dartington, or Spiegelau are almost certain to do the trick.

Wine buffs are in universal agreement that the right glass will concentrate and enhance the flavor of the wine by directing its flow to the right taste zones of the mouth. It will also intensify and capture the aromas when you nose it. Suddenly, an average bottle you picked up from the convenience store on your way home from work will taste as though you've spent double that amount. Think this sounds like hocus-pocus? Buy just one glass, then taste the same bottle of wine in a pub-style Paris goblet and in the hand-blown upstart. The difference will astonish you.

HOW LOW CAN YOU GO?

Nobody likes paying tax, especially not on their wine, but, unfortunately, the fun-sapping tax man is happy to take a hefty cut from every single bottle sold. This means that once you've factored in the cost of bottling and shipping your $8 (£5) vino, only a few cents of the retail price actually go toward the liquid itself. This means that there is such a thing as a too-cheap bottle. If you've forked out less than five dollars, all you've really spent money on is tax and transport, but as soon as you spend more than that—even a couple of bucks—then you'll find the quality of what's in your bottle increases dramatically. So for the best value, don't go for the bargain bin.

So where are the best deals? Generally speaking, they're to be found at supermarkets, where most people buy their wine. Supermarket wine buyers wield enormous power. They have the ability to negotiate amazing deals with their suppliers, who covet a place on their shelves. You should still approach such deals with a degree of skepticism, though—would you have paid full price for the bottle, or could it have been marked up to begin with? Keep an eye on the newspaper columnists' advice. They get prior notice of all the discounts going into stores and can do the legwork in picking out the decent bottles so you don't have to.

THE BEST CELLARS

Almost all wine is consumed on the day we buy it. In the US, the industry reckons that 95 per cent of wine is opened within 15 minutes of it leaving the store—fast work! However, cellaring wine—storing it until it reaches perfect maturity—is a good way to avoid having to pay over the odds for a specific

By all means stock up when you see a good offer on a personal favorite wine, but maintain a level of caution if an offer seems too good to be true—it quite possibly is.

vintage. If you are buying wine for an investment that you intend to resell, it is invariably better to pay for professional, insured storage. Not only will it make your wine more attractive to future buyers, but it will also prevent you from accidentally uncorking the wrong bottle.

The good news is that cellaring wine doesn't require an actual cellar—after all, they're hardly practical in a second-floor apartment—but in order for the wine to remain in good condition, you will need to re-create the cool and stable environment of a cellar. The very worst place to store wine for any longer than a couple of days is the kitchen because of the temperature fluctuations. Instead, if you have some cash to throw at the problem, invest in a temperature- and humidity-controlled cabinet. If you don't have the money or the space, then buy polystyrene packing containers (the ones specifically designed to protect wine in the mail). Mark the packages with the bottles' drink-by date (the tasting notes should give you an estimated range) and tuck them away somewhere they won't be disturbed—under the bed in the spare room, for example—until they're ready. Just make sure that thirsty guests don't go hunting for a nightcap.

CHAPTER 3

BEER AND A DROP OF CIDER, TOO

Beer is currently experiencing its most significant decade since man first mashed up hops and water together around 4,000 years ago. While at gigs, festivals, clubs, and down-at-heel bars across the globe, you're still likely to be left staring despondently into the bottom of a plastic glass of flat lager, wondering how you managed to hand over a fiver for its insipid contents, but elsewhere a craft revolution is underway. Thanks to the commendable work of a new generation of brewers sick of dull, low-quality drinks, beer has become tastier, more varied, artisan-produced, and way more interesting than the mass-market lagers to which we've sadly become accustomed. Following the pioneering efforts of US microbreweries, the craft beer phenomenon is spreading everywhere from Sydney to Stockholm and Rome to Rio. Oh, and fear not, the real-ale and cask-conditioned-beer geeks are nowhere in sight.

BORN IN BOSTON

To unearth the roots of the current craze for small-batch beer, we need to head to mid-Eighties Boston, specifically to Jim Koch's kitchen where, while everyone else was busy learning how to moonwalk to Billie Jean, Koch was reviving an old family recipe for lager. It turns out those pre-Prohibition brewers knew what they were about, and the recipe tasted so good that the Samuel Adams brand was born.

While Samuel Adams might not have been the first craft brewery—that honor goes to the New Albion Brewing Company in Sonoma, California—its award for Best Beer in America at the 1985 Great American Beer Festival helped to open a lot of eyes that something interesting was happening in the brewing world. The brewery's success was almost certainly a reaction against the bland and low-alcohol beers that the market was awash with, and it sparked a chain reaction of small-scale, high-quality brewers establishing themselves across the US. There were 2,360 at the last count. Although in the UK and Europe there had always been real ale and Belgian and German beers to add interest to the market, the lager sector had become increasingly bland, driven by corporate brands determined to dominate, rather than by flavor. And it's this part of the industry that, inspired by what was happening in the States, has since taken things up a level.

"Squirrel beer? Whoever came up with this idea is clearly nuts!"

In Scotland, a young, loud-mouthed company called BrewDog—a self-styled "punk" brewer—set itself the task of re-energizing the UK's beer market. BrewDog's first beer—essentially a really tasty lager sold out of the back of a van—quickly got a lot of people's attention. Everything that came next, from the world's strongest beer to a bottle housed in a stuffed squirrel, caused international outrage, and a lot of publicity. Underpinning the stunts, though, were a couple of excellent hand-crafted beers, and punters voted with their wallets. BrewDog is now one of Scotland's most successful enterprises, exporting its beers across the globe, and the owners even have their own TV show in the US.

Meanwhile, a plethora of equally inspired (although maybe not so ADHD) companies sprang up, bringing their craft products to the market. Although Britain's beer has never been entirely dominated by the big boys—independent pubs have always had real ales on their pumps—the difference is that the UK's craft movement is taking root right in the heart of what should be the mass-market's consumer base. It's the young lager drinkers who are demanding more. It's good for beer and it's good for business (brewers and pubs alike, as we shall see).

Canned beer

Further proof of the slightly irreverent, preconception-shaking nature of craft beer is summed up by its recent move into the canned beer market. Formerly the reserve of the very cheapest lagers and the brands usually favored by hobos and tramps, cans are now the coolest way to drink your beer. Back in 2002, the Colorado-based Oskar Blues brewery decided that the new water-based coating that lined aluminum cans would prevent any kind of tinny taste from entering their beer. The cans also stop light getting to the beer, and are a rock-solid seal against any air creeping into the brew. The craft can market is now massive in the US and a growing force in the UK. Whether you're in a hip downtown bar or an upmarket burger chain, you can be sure that craft cans will be on the menu.

TIME FOR A BREW

So what differentiates a craft brewer from a more commercial operation? It's not just a question of scale—although in America a craft brewer must produce less than six million barrels of beer per year—but rather a question of quality, tradition, and independence. Proper beer (ale or lager) should contain only four ingredients: malted barley, hops, water, and yeast. In Germany, all beers are governed by the 1516 Reinheitsgebot purity rules, which enforce this, but the commercial operations in other countries aren't as restricted in what ingredients they are allowed to use. These breweries look to cut costs and use other grains called adjuncts—corn, rice, rye, oats, and wheat—which can be added to the recipe, bulking up the volume and alcohol but without contributing to flavor or style.

For craft brews, the barley must be "malted" to release the sugars from the grain, and these sugars are then fermented. To do this, the germination process is started by wetting the grains, which release their sugars. Germination is then stopped by toasting the grain. This heating process is key to the flavor of the resulting beer: the more it's cooked, the more intense the brew.

Next up are the hops. These are actually female flowers harvested from a vine that's a distant relation of marijuana (but without the psychoactive side effects). Depending on the variety selected—a century-old Dutch plant or a new brewer's mash-up—the hops give flavor, natural preservatives, and bitterness to the liquid. Hops are varietal, which means a hop grown in the Czech Republic will have a different flavor from one grown in the southeast of England.

The final taste component is the yeast. Just as sourdough bread can taste different because of the personality and characteristics of the yeast used, so too can beer. Because each microorganism is unique, brewers are as protective of their yeast stock as they would be of a teenage daughter. Ale yeasts tend to deliver more flavor than lager yeasts, as they ferment at warmer temperatures, and release fruity flavor compounds called esters that give Belgian beers in particular an aroma of banana or citrus. These warmer temperatures also mean that ale matures faster than lager— the name comes from the German word *lagern*, which means "to store."

HOP VARIETIES

There are four main hop-growing regions around the world:

North America: The northwest states of Oregon and Washington are the center of the US hop industry. They are famous for producing varieties such as Citra, Cascade, and Columbus, which are grouped together under the name C-hops. It is their citrus flavor profile that gives US Pale Ales and IPAs their distinctive bitter taste. This flavor, perhaps more than any other, is the one that is used to great effect in some of the most famous examples of craft beer, including Sierra Nevada Pale Ale and BrewDog Punk IPA.

South Pacific: South Australia and New Zealand produce a range of hops including Nelson Sauvin, Motueka, and Galaxy. The flavors of these varieties have elements of tropical fruits including mango and passion fruit, which give the local brews a very distinctive taste that other brewers across the world are keen to try to replicate.

United Kingdom: English hop varieties including Fuggles, Goldings, and Challenger will always be associated with traditional English bitters, but don't let misguided preconceptions of warm English beer put you off. Their distinctive floral characteristics, spicy elements, and echoes of hedgerow and orchard fruit make them a versatile and popular choice for pale ales, stouts, and porters.

Central Europe: Noble hops is the name given to the varieties grown mainly in Germany and the Czech Republic. There are four noble hop varieties: Tettnang, Spalt, Hallertau, and Saaz. These are the hops found in classic Bavarian and Bohemian beer styles such as Pilsner, Helles, and Bock, as well as in Belgian Trappist and Pale Ales.

YEAST STOCK - NO ENTRY!

To turn these ingredients into beer, first the malted barley is crushed and mixed with warm water to extract all the fermentable sugars. The resulting liquid is then boiled, along with the hops for bitterness, to make the "wort." Depending on the flavor the brewer is trying to create, more hops may be added toward the end of the boil at a lower temperature to release their more delicate (floral, citrusy) flavor and aroma molecules. The spent grain husks are separated off, and the wort is then fermented with yeast, which causes carbon dioxide (CO_2) to be released, making the bubbles in your beer. It can then be cask conditioned (real ale), when it will undergo a secondary fermentation in the pub's cellar before it can be served, or simply conditioned, pasteurized, and packed off as draft beer.

THERE'S MORE TO BEER THAN LAGER

It's not surprising, considering we've been whipping up beer since Neanderthal times, that a huge variety of different styles have emerged across the globe. In the UK, the most common are lager (the standard session beer); mild ale (which means lightly hopped rather than not alcoholic); bitter (lots of hops, rich color); golden (aimed to wean lager drinkers onto ale); IPA (strong, hop-rich India Pale Ale at over 4 per cent); and stout. Porter (named after the market porters who drank it by the gallon) and stout (a stronger version of porter) were originally made in London in the early eighteenth century. They are a blend of stale or "aged" beer with fresh mild porter. In 1759, Arthur Guinness decided to launch an Irish version, and the country's biggest export was founded; 1.5 billion pints of the black stuff are now sold worldwide each year. Sláinte.

Belgium is also a world leader when it comes to beer styles. It is famous for its Trappist and Abbey brews, which fall into two main categories—dubbels and tripels—but a visit to a Belgian beer bar will also uncover blonde ales, fruit beers, seasonal farmhouse ales, wheat beers, and other curiosites including lambic, gueze, and sour beers.

Further east, the Germans and Czechs are responsible for the development of lager in the form of bitter pilsner, lighter helles, and strong bock lagers, as well as darker Dunkel and Schwarzbiers, and Weißbiers made from wheat.

All these varieties, along with the historic ties to European immigrants, have made US brewers weak at the knees, as they experiment with different styles to create their own unique take on beer. The most celebrated example is the US IPA, arguably the most popular and enduring craft beer style.

APPLES AND PEARS

Historically associated with the UK but gradually gaining recognition on a global scale, cider, or zider as it is more correctly pronounced in the West Country of England where it is traditionally made, is one of the most underrated alcoholic drinks. Given its gloriously simple nature—essentially just pressed and fermented apples—it seems odd that anyone would want to add water, yeast, sugar, and preservatives. However, the economics of big-scale cider mean that there can be as little as 35 per cent apple juice in your glass, and you can get all kinds of drink under the "cider" label. Whether you like to throw ice into a fizzy pint of it or whether you love the more natural farm-gate product, the best thing is that cider's star is rising, and that means more choice and better quality.

A friendly word of warning: if you're in a bar in the US and you want to drink cider, make sure you ask for hard cider, otherwise you'll be left with a rather disappointing glass of alcohol-free apple juice.

TRADITIONAL CIDER

In its most unadulterated form, traditional alcoholic cider is called scrumpy; made with pears, it's known as perry. The apples used are generally bitter-sweet and bitter-sharp varieties, which, because of their high tannin levels, don't taste good for eating. The fruit ripens in the fall when, conveniently, the cooler days are perfect for apple-pressing. Once the harvest is in, the apples are milled (squashed up a bit) and the resulting pulp is layered with straw or wooden slats in a block called a cheese. This is then pressed to extract all the juicy goodness.

The West Country of England: great for cider, not so great on fashion choices.

Now, if nature were left to run its course uninhibited, the natural yeast on the fruits' skin would begin the fermentation process. However, since this means there are also bacteria present, it can result in a slightly funky cider. While in farm-made scrumpy, wild fermentation is the norm, on a commercial scale, the yeast, sugar levels, and fermentation are all carefully (though artificially) controlled, and a little sulfur dioxide (SO_2) is added to the product to keep any bacterial nasties at bay during fermentation.

Traditional cider is usually left to ferment over winter, although in the UK it may be disturbed briefly for some traditional "wassailing" in January to bless the orchards. Then, when spring's warmer weather comes, the yeast wakes up again to finish its work. In big-scale operations, the cider is then pasteurized to make sure no further fermentation takes place. Scrumpy's lethally boozy reputation is perhaps a result of the fact that it's unpasteurized, which means the yeast isn't killed off and its alcohol content is still liable to creep up once the drink is bottled or put into vats.

Whichever raw ingredient is chosen, it's first mashed up and fermented to produce a base, beer-like liquid that can be distilled to capture the alcohol. The distillation happens in two ways, either by using a column still (the method favored by commercial operations—picture an oil refinery) or with a pot still (which is more usual for single malt whisky production or artisan spirits, where flavor is king). Both use the same principle: the alcohol is evaporated off at 78.5°C (173.3°F), then cooled and collected. The "heads" (the first compounds to be evaporated) and the "tails" (the last) are removed, to ensure only a clean "cut" of spirit, known as the heart, is bottled.

The producer then decides whether to filter the vodka to remove any impurities—and also any flavor molecules—before adding water to bring it down to a palatable proof, about 40 per cent ABV. If you're drinking it chilled and neat (and why not, indeed?), then filtration is worth paying attention to, because it alters the "feel" of the vodka in your mouth. Charcoal is said to produce a crisp, light spirit, while filtration using silver or platinum makes for a thicker, creamier spirit. If you want to compare and contrast, then try Russian Standard Platinum—a fine example of precious-metal filtration—and a measure of France's Grey Goose, which is lightly filtered to retain as much of the wheat flavor as possible. Both are delicious and surprisingly different.

So, when—wallet in hand at the airport Duty Free—you're trying to decide which bottle to take to the checkout, remember that the ingredients, distillation method (it's likely to be mentioned on the label if it's small-batch, pot-distilled), and filtration are what actually affect the quality and taste of the spirit. Packaging only affects how much change you get back.

GIN

If vodka is the simplest and purest of the spirits, then its more complicated sibling is gin. Gin is essentially a flavored vodka: a neutral spirit that has been infused with various natural botanicals (flowers, spices, and fruits) to add herbal, floral, spicy, and citrusy characteristics. It is a direct descendent of Dutch genever, which was first sold as medicine in the 1600s and originally made from distilled malt wine, mixed with herbs and juniper berries to mask its unpleasant taste. Once gin landed on British shores, Londoners took to it with gusto. The city was sloshing with the stuff, and gin shops sprang up on every corner. In those days, the spirit would have had little resemblance to the gin we drink now: it was sweetened to hide the roughness of the alcohol, and often served with peppermint to soothe the stomach (something of a vicious circle, eh?).

Following on from this gin-soaked era, the quality of the base spirit was improved, so less sugar and fewer flavorings were used. Brands such as Gordon's were formed in the mid-1700s, creating a style known as "London Dry." The name is 50 per cent misleading, as it doesn't have to be distilled in London, but there are a few rules for its manufacture, namely that it must be made from neutral spirit and certain botanicals must be added, and it must be distilled with no added sugar.

So, these "botanicals"—what are they? Well, by law they must include juniper berries, and after that, it is the maker's choice. Typical recipes include cilantro, or coriander (which gives a lemon flavor);

angelica root (which acts as a kind of binding agent); licorice, or liquorish, root; and chamomile flowers. Some gins use as few as four botanicals, while others blend more than 40. In the past few years, as gin's reputation and popularity have exploded, distillers have started experimenting with new botanicals. Hendrick's, which uses cucumber and rose petals, is probably the most deliberately different gin. Those in the know drink it with a slice of cucumber, rather than lime, to enhance the botanicals' flavors. Tanqueray, on the other hand, is at the simplest and most balanced end of the market, with just four botanicals in the mix.

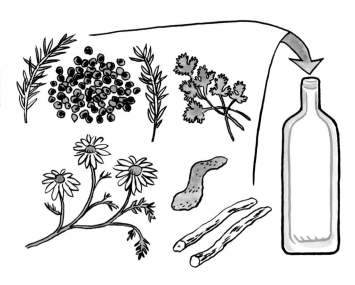

Popular botanicals used to infuse gins include (clockwise from top left) rosemary, juniper berries, lavender, cilantro (coriander), angelica root, licorice root, lemon peel, and chamomile.

Once the quality of the botanicals has been checked—often by women, as they are considered to have more sensitive noses—distillation can take place. This is when a very high-quality, neutral-flavored grain alcohol is put into the pot still along with the flowers and berries. When the spirit runs off the still, it can be called gin, and it's ready to bottle, ship to bars, and serve.

If you're going to slosh a lot of cheap tonic into your gin, then chances are you won't be able to identify any individual flavors, aside from the familiar pine-tree smell of juniper. In a martini, however, you'll quickly find that the quality and subtleties of your gin—its dryness, floral notes, and citrus flavor—make a huge difference. Once you start looking, you'll quickly find the character of gin you prefer. For example, Bombay Sapphire was deliberately designed to be a mild gin—it's not copper-pot distilled and it "passes through" the botanicals, rather than being left in contact with them—to try to lure us away from previously favored vodka. At the other end of the spectrum, you'll find gins such as Tanqueray Ten and Sipsmith, which are laden with wonderful botanical character and are unmistakably excellent examples of the spirit. Tanqueray Ten has grapefruit in its recipe, so a real aficionado would ask for their martini to be served with a twist of grapefruit (preferably white).

"I like to have a Martini,
two at the very most;
three, I'm under the table,
four, I'm under my host."
DOROTHY PARKER

TEQUILA

The most maligned and misunderstood of spirits is tequila—did you just gag? We have used and abused it, throwing it down in shots—and probably throwing it up again just as quickly—but there is way more to tequila than you might think. It's made from agave, which is not a cactus, as often thought, but a relative of the lily. If you want to drink decent tequila, it should say 100 per cent agave on the label, not "mixto," which means that up to 49 per cent of other sugars may have been used. The making of tequila is geographically controlled, and can take place only in certain parts of Jalisco, Mexico, where tequila was first produced by the Spanish conquistadors.

Once ripe, the heart of the agave plant is harvested and cooked to transform the starch into sugars. These baked pinas are then pressed or mashed to extract the juice, which is put into vats to be fermented before being distilled twice. The resulting spirit is called blanco tequila. In this unaged form, it tastes vegetal, fresh, sometimes citrusy, and can easily be sipped and savored, especially with food. Salt and lemon need not apply.

The "tequila" worm is actually a myth. They are only ever found in certain bottles of mezcal produced in the state of Oaxaca.

....

Old enough to taste better

When the blanco is a couple of months old, we enter the lesser-known world of aged tequila. The categories are: reposado ("rested"—aged between two months and a year); añejo (between one and three years); and extra añejo (more than three years). Cynics might argue that this last category was invented in 2006 for the super-premium brands wanting a more exclusive classification.

Tequila is aged in oak, often the hand-me-down barrels from the whisky industry, which gives it more complex flavors, such as sweet vanilla, and a caramel color. Reposado and añejo tequilas become increasingly mellow and sippable as they age, with some of that vegetal freshness giving way to more whisky-like caramel and spice notes. Taste your way through a couple of different brands to find which characteristics and ages work best for you.

One thing that should be noticeably absent from your tequila bottle is worms. Not only are they a marketing gimmick for tourists, but also they are only usually found in mezcal (the Mr. Hyde to tequila's Dr. Jekyll). Mezcal may look like tequila, and smell a bit like it, too, but it is actually a brawling, smoking, volatile relation that's made without any of the same production regulations. This doesn't mean all mezcal is bad—in fact, it is currently enjoying "bartenders' favorite" status—but just ensure you approach it with caution.

TEQUILA

"There's naught, no doubt, so much the spirit calms as rum and true religion."

LORD BYRON

RUM

Yes, there's something of Club Tropicana and the cocktail umbrella about rum. And, yes, it carries connotations of pirates and reeling sailors and Johnny Depp wearing eyeliner—but so what? We don't have to take all spirits seriously. Rum-makers are governed by few rules and many exceptions, creating spirits that span everything from barely-there light rums to dark and stormy black spirits.

Slavers, traders, and pirates introduced the world to this "hot and vile liquor" back in the seventeenth century, when they unearthed its spiritual home in the lush Caribbean islands and Latin America, where it emerged as a by-product of the sugar industry. Such was its influence that it was only in 1970, on "Black Tot Day," that the Royal Navy ended its daily rum-ration for sailors (alarming to think that those in charge of war frigates may have been over the limit, eh?).

Depending on the history of the island producing it, rum is made from either sugar-cane juice (known as rhum agricole, which is typical of the French-colonized islands) or cooked sugar-cane molasses (rhum industriel), which accounts for around 90 per cent of the world's rum.

To make rhum industriel, blackstrap molasses—which is a bit like treacle—is mixed with water to reduce the sugar content, before being fermented and distilled. The less concentrated sugar-cane juice of rhum agricole can be fermented without adding water. The length of fermentation and the amount of aging are the twin factors that influence the style of rum made.

Under the hot, hot Caribbean sun, spirits age in dog years—many times faster than their Scotch counterparts—as the intense heat speeds evaporation. The warm spirit is drawn into the barrel's porous wood, where it picks up both flavor and color. As with tequila, different amounts of aging produce different styles of rum. White (or light) rum, such as Bacardi Superior, is a useful neutral base for cocktails, as it's barely aged and is filtered to remove any color.

While the pineapple might look impressive to you, it's not going to leave a good impression on more seasoned drinkers.

RUM

Pick a color

Next up is golden rum, which has more complex flavors (caramel, baked bananas, coconut, and so on), and it's usually made from a blend of different aged rums. It's an excellent style to experiment with, but beware of cheap bottles that have been colored artificially with caramel, rather than being properly aged. The heaviest rums are navy, or dark, rums. Although these get a degree of their tar-like color and tannic taste from the barrel-aging, they also have molasses added to give them extra richness. These are probably best served with a sea-shanty.

The less common rum categories are only-just-legal overproof, when the rum is bottled at cask strength, and spiced rum, which is essentially a flavored, sweetened spirit. A big area for growth at the premium end of the industry is "age statement" rums, where the label says how long the youngest spirit in its blend has been matured for. This is a healthy sign that the rum industry is trying to establish something like the connoisseurs' market that exists for single malt whisky. In recent years, this has meant that some brilliant new brands have arrived on the scene. So whether you prefer pina coladas served in pineapples or a Hemingway-style daiquiri, there is a rum to suit all tastes.

WHISK(E)Y

Whisk(e)y is one of those spirits that's a true product of its place: while one dram might have the delicate caress of heather and honey, another can smack you around the chops with the reek of brine, sea-lashed shores, and rain-soaked peat. Finding your perfect whisk(e)y could be a life's work (and one well spent, many would argue). Before we get too involved, it's worth mentioning that extra "e." While no one is too sure of its origins, Irish and American whiskeys will always use it on their labels. Those from the UK (most famously, Scotland), Japan, and Canada will all be labeled as whisky.

100 per cent pure?

There are two different categories of whisky to investigate: blends and single malts. Blended whisky accounts for more than 90 per cent of the industry and can be anything from a supermarket own-brand through to the masterful Johnnie Walker Blue at the upper end of the price spectrum. In the same way that a Champagne-maker combines different wines to maintain their house flavor, so, too, the master blender at a distillery must mix different whiskies to create his product. A combination of various single malts and grain whiskies is used—some recipes will ask for a dozen or so ingredients, while others call for more than 40 different whiskies—all of which must come together in a consistent style. That's no mean feat when you consider that no two barrels in a warehouse are identical.

As the name implies, a single malt is a whisky that's made from just one grain (malted barley) and in Scotland—where the best are made—there are a fair few rules that govern its production. First, the barley needs to be malted, which is when germination is started so that the grain begins to release its sugars. When the grain has the right amount of sugar, germination is stopped by warming it in a kiln. This also adds extra smoky and peat flavors (known as phenols) to the grain. The barley is then ground up to a flour—the grist—and mixed with the second vital ingredient—water. Whether this is from a pure mountain stream or a peat-rich loch, it will have a massive effect on the taste of the whisky. The grist and water mix—the wort—is then fermented with yeast to make a beer-like liquid, which is distilled twice. As with some gins, single malt distillation takes place in copper pot stills, all of which tend to have their own personality: their shape, size, and any lumps and bumps will influence the taste of the new-make spirit they produce. When the spirit is cooled and condensed and begins to run off the still, it comes out clear. It won't be called whisky until it has been aged for at least three years in barrels.

In the dark and cool of bonded warehouses, the real alchemy takes place. Hundreds of oak casks filled with spirit rest, while each stave of wood plays its part in forming the character of the spirit it hosts. Having first been used by bourbon or sherry producers, these secondhand barrels made of white oak (*Quercus alba*), with their charred insides and unique flavors, are the last part of the whisky's recipe. As subtle changes in temperature draw the spirit into the wood, it picks up a golden color and toasted, sweet, vanilla notes. Under the watchful eye of the warehouse workers, the spirit ages, drawing more and more flavor compounds from the wood, and enriching itself to become increasingly complex and mellow. This maturation can last longer than it

HOW TO TASTE

But what about the actual taste of whisky? How do you drink it? Is adding ice sacrilegious? What about drinking it with food? And how on earth do you decide which dram to order anyway? First, we'll deal with how, then we'll move on to what. Remember that taste is entirely subjective, so there is no "right way" to drink whisky, other than the method you like best. A classic whisky-tasting glass looks like a miniature wine glass, with enough room for swirling the spirit, while the flavors are trapped by the narrow opening at the top.

1 Approach your dram neat. Give it a swirl, then have a short, sharp sniff—your nose will need to acclimatize to the alcohol—before going back in for another. Think about what you can smell: mild antiseptic (TCP), brine, coconut, honey, vanilla, spice, fruit—your nose is primed to pick up the real character of the spirit.

2 Now have a sip. Roll it around your whole tongue and let it melt like chocolate, so that you can pick up all the flavors—breathe in through your mouth so your sense of smell can help you taste. Does it stay with you, and do more flavors emerge? Or does it disappear as soon as you've swallowed? Try to judge its length and complexity.

3 Next, add a splash of water—just a few drops. The Scots call this "releasing the serpent" (maybe don't repeat this to the girl next to you at the bar), and you'll see the oils in the whisky reacting with the H2O. If the whisky is unfiltered, it may go cloudy. Fear not, this isn't a fault with your dram. It's meant to happen. A whole raft of different aromas and flavors should hit you: light and floral or smoky and heavy. Sit back, relax, and savor them.

takes to have a child, raise it, and support it through several years at university—which makes the fifty you paid for a bottle of 18-year-old Glenfiddich suddenly seem excellent value.

Finding the right whisky

The question of which whisky you'll like is a tricky one, and if you think you don't like whisky, chances are you just haven't found the right one yet. There are some characteristics that are associated with the region where the whisky's made; the Islands (Islay—pronounced "i-lar"—is the most famous) tend to make wild, peaty, sea-influenced drams; examples from the Lowlands tend to be light and fruit-filled; Speyside whiskies are typically sweeter; while the Highland region is so large that its whiskies are hard to generalize. But each bottling has its own characteristics, and one distillery can produce a huge range of styles, which is all part of the fun of single malt.

One of the best ways to start finding out what you like is to work through whisky expert Dave Broom's Flavour Map (just type that into Google). This plots out how light/rich and how delicate/smoky some of the most famous brands are on an x-y axis. You'll soon work out whether you're more drawn to the apples, lemon, and floral notes of a Dalwhinnie or the unctuous peaty weight of a Lagavulin 16-year-old. Or it may just be a question of what you're drinking it with—the lighter styles of whisky are a perfect match with shellfish, while some of the richer, more coffee/tobacco/spice-flavored drams are possibly the best accompaniment to chocolate there is going.

"There is no bad whiskey. There are only some whiskeys that aren't as good as others."
RAYMOND CHANDLER

BOURBON

Kentucky isn't just famous for Colonel Sanders' chicken: the state's other celebrated export is Bourbon whiskey, and it's every bit as finger-lickin' good. Made from corn grown in vast, sun-baked fields, Bourbon was originally made as a way of using up unwanted grains. There are some pretty stringent laws that regulate what can go into it. First the mash bill—the grain recipe—must contain at least 51 per cent corn, and the rest a combination of rye (the "flavor" grain), wheat (for creaminess), and barley. It must be distilled by one of the seven distilleries in the state of Kentucky to below 80% ABV before it goes on to be matured in new American oak barrels for a minimum of two years. Remember that the wood is a massively important part of the recipe, and American oak is particularly rich in vanillin oils, which give those lovely vanilla and butterscotch flavors.

The intense summer heat and cold winters of Kentucky mean that the spirit ages much faster than Scottish whisky: the hot weather expands the spirit, pushing it into the wood's pores, then, through the winter, the cold drives it back out to rest. The angels' share (the amount evaporated from each cask) is staggering. Walk past a warehouse on a hot day and the air is laced with the smell of the spirit—around 50 per cent of a cask will be lost over a 15-year aging. It's not surprising, then, that most Bourbons are bottled at a relatively young age compared with Scotch. After all, no one wants to see the heavenly host too sloshed.

Taste-wise, Bourbon is pretty sweet—if it were a breakfast, it would be maple syrup and bacon pancakes—and it's an amazing match with barbecue, pulled pork, or sticky ribs. It is also one of the best cocktail spirits out there. Brands to look

The American Distilling Institute estimates that every year 3–4 per cent of the contents of a barrel evaporates as the angels' share.

out for include the small-batch Woodford Reserve, Maker's Mark, and, at the top end of the category, George T. Stagg, which reaches parts other whiskeys can only dream of. Just don't mix it with Coke.

Tennessee whiskey

This brings us on to possibly the most famous whiskey with an "e" in it: Jack Daniel's. It's made in a similar way to Bourbon, but because the Gentleman hails from the neighboring dry state of Tennessee, and is filtered through charcoal, it's called a Tennessee whiskey. There's not much point in going into the flavor of JD, because you'll be mixing it with coke anyhow, right?

Rye

Last, but not least, comes American Rye whiskey. This spicy, peppery spirit traditionally hails from Maryland and Pennsylvania, where the first Irish and Scottish immigrants set up shop. Although almost all the great American cocktails owe their humble origins to Rye whiskey—this is where the Manhattan and the old fashioned began—Bourbon pushed it out of favor, being smoother, sweeter, and generally less rambunctious. Now, though, the battle for supremacy is on, and premium ryes are increasingly muscling their way back into bars. If you like a punchy mouthful, then brands to look out for include Rittenhouse, Van Winkle, and Sazerac.

COGNAC

Pull a chair up to the fire, light a cigar, and pour yourself a brandy... Actually, scratch that. Paunch-sporting, gray-head status is no longer required for Cognac-drinking, not now that it's the go-to accessory for Busta Rhymes, Snoop Dogg, Kanye West, et al.

Distilled from wine, Cognac, the king of French brandies, is an appellation contrôlé product, named for the town at the center of the region where it's made, near Bordeaux. The best Cognacs are made from the grapes grown in the Grande and Petite Champagne regions (the only relation to the sparkling wine is the etymology; the name comes from the French for "chalky soil").

The white grapes are pressed and made into a disgusting-tasting wine, which is perfect for distilling—its high acidity translates to flavors that age really well. Once it's been through the Charentais still (a legally controlled size and shape of pot still, first imported by the Dutch in the

The rapper Ludacris enjoys drinking Cognac, or 'yak, so much that he launched his own blend, Conjure.

seventeenth century), the spirit is aged in Limousin oak casks for a minimum of two years before blending and bottling. There are different grades of Cognac: VS (very special); VSOP (very special old pale); and XO (extra old, which must be aged for at least six years). The categories are named in English because the Brits were—and still are—the biggest market for Cognac. Almost 100 per cent of what is made is exported, as the French tend to favor Cognac's lesser-known cousin Armagnac (same idea, different region). Makes you wonder what we might be missing out on, doesn't it?

"Cognac is the drink that's drank by G's."
SNOOP DOGG

CHAPTER 5

HOW TO BUILD YOUR HOME LIQUOR CABINET

crisp; rosso, which is ruby-red and bitter; and bianco, which is the sweetest of the lot. Vermouths are a great way to add bitterness and herbal complexity to a cocktail, and are essential for classics such as martinis and negronis, or when served long, Mediterranean-style, with soda and ice.

Bitters—you know, that curious, paper-wrapped bottle of Angostura on your grandmother's drinks shelf—were originally concocted by monks and herbalists who were in search of cures for all manner of ailments. They are made by distilling a (usually top-secret) combination of roots, herbs, fruits, and flowers in a base spirit to formulate a potent tincture, which can be either aromatic, citrus-based, or a "pouring bitter," such as Italian favorites Campari and Aperol.

Their role in the cocktail is to sharpen and heighten your senses—like upgrading your analog TV to high-definition digital—and to enhance all the flavors in the drink. While the oldest recipes on the market hail from the early 1800s, in the past couple of years, there has been a huge revival of interest in bitters, resulting in the creation of enticing new brands. Try companies such as the Bitter Truth and Fee Brothers, or head to the nearest decent cocktail joint to find out what the bartenders are cooking up for themselves.

TOOLS TO BUY (AND HOW TO MAKE DO)

You are going to need some kit. The first of each of the items below is the professional choice. Following that is a suggested alternative that may be lurking in the kitchen cupboard somewhere, but will definitely be good enough for you to improvise with and start shaking right now.

Pro: **Boston shaker**

This is a much more practical way to
mix a cocktail than the old-fashioned-
looking shakers that come in three
parts. One beaker is made of glass,
so you can see the drink being
mixed, while the other is robust tin, ideal for
mashing or muddling.

Impro: **Glass jar**

Don't forget the lid, or this could get messy.

Pro: **Hawthorne strainer**

Since the Boston shaker doesn't have a built-in
strainer, you'll definitely need one of these. It
fits over the tin beaker, and as you pour the
mixture through it, it will filter out any pieces
of ice, fruit, and foliage that you don't want to
tip into the glass.

Impro: **Sieve**

This should do the trick.

Pro: **Fine strainer**

Some drinks call for more refined treatment, and need all the ice
chips strained. This is where a mini sieve comes into play.

Impro: **Coffee filter paper**

Alternatively, tip your cocktail into a (very clean) French press
(cafetière) and plunge it.

Pro: Bar spoon

This cheap and innocuous-looking item will prove endlessly useful. It's perfect for measuring the smallest ingredient quantities (1 tsp/5ml serves), and you can use its flat end for crushing soft fruit or (advanced level) layering drinks.

Impro: **Um, a normal spoon**

Teaspoon-size for measuring, and a long-handled spoon for swizzling.

Pro: Muddler

Although "muddling" may sound like a bartender's term for confusing customers, it actually refers to the process of crushing fruit or herbs to extract their juices and oils. Traditionally, a wooden muddler is used (wood is both strong and hygienic), although once it would have been a piece of sugar cane.

Impro: **Small rolling pin**

Use the end of a small rolling pin, or the pestle from your mortar and pestle.

Pro: **Measure (jigger)**

Making cocktails is like mixing a cake batter: getting the quantities just right is essential. And while some professionals prefer to free-pour their spirits (they count the bubbles to ensure accuracy), this requires practice and constant testing to make sure you've got your eye in. Instead, cocktail-making is far easier if you stick to using a measure, preferably dual-sided, with a ¾oz (25ml) serve on one end and a 1½oz (50ml) serve on the other.

Impro: **Measuring spoons**

If you have a set of these, they'll do the job. Otherwise, raid the kitchen drawers: a dessertspoon holds around 10ml, and a teaspoon 5ml.

Pro: **Manual citrus press**

These are incredibly useful, easy to clean, and cheap to buy. To use, simply slice your fruit in half (do this when it's at room temperature—you'll get more juice), put the cut side down in the press, and flip the handle over to squeeze it.

Impro: **Squeeze by hand**

Roll the fruit before cutting in two. This helps release the juices. If you have a piece of muslin, cover the halved fruit and squeeze it into a bowl. If not, just spear it with a fork and twist it to get as much liquid as possible.

Pro: **Paring knife**

Keep a little knife to hand for prepping garnish, peeling zest, or slicing fruit.

Impro: **Sharp knife**

Come on, you do have one, right?

Pro: **Selection of glasses**

Glassware makes a huge difference to the experience of drinking a cocktail. For wine, the glass can actually change the way you taste and smell the liquid, but for mixed drinks, it can alter the way the ice melts, the drink's temperature, and—most significant of all—the aesthetics. Ideally, you will have three styles: highball glass (tall, for long, iced drinks); rocks glass (squat, for serving short cocktails or neat spirits over ice); and classic martini glass (make sure it's not too large or the drink will warm up before you've had time to drink it—a 5oz/150ml glass is plenty big enough).

Impro: **Time to get creative**

Hollow out fruit, use old glass jars, dig out your old tin camping mugs, recycle (very well-washed) paint cans, raid the cupboards—all the best bars are using quirky glassware, so don't hold back.

GET THE ICE RIGHT

No matter how much care you've taken to source the most buttery vodka and the most fragrant gin, your drinks will be undone in seconds if you mix them using ice that smells of something, especially fish. Ice needs to be as fresh as possible, to prevent it being tainted by other occupants of your freezer. It should also—and this sounds obvious—be really, really stick-to-your-fingers cold, rather than slippery and thawing. Wet ice over-dilutes drinks.

If you're buying ice, look for the largest solid cubes possible (ideally without a pocket of air or hole in them). If you're making your own, consider using filtered water if the water from your faucet is very chlorinated or chalky. Also, boil it before you freeze it—this reduces the amount of air that is trapped in the water when it freezes, making denser, colder ice.

Another impressive trick comes courtesy of a new gadget on the market: round ice-cube molds. These allow you to make tennis ball-sized spheres, which dilute more slowly because of their lower surface area to quantity of ice ratio (type "Sphere Ice Molds" into Google). They're ideal for whisky or cocktails such as an old fashioned.

ESSENTIAL COCKTAILS

There are three cocktails that you should know how to mix.

DRY MARTINI

As with all the classics, the origins of this drink are lost in the mist of alcohol-soaked time. It's thought to be an evolution of the martinez (see chapter 6), and is attributed by some to a bartender called Martini di Arma di Taggia, who was working in New York in 1912. No matter how it got here, we're glad it did.

INGREDIENTS

2oz/4 tbsp (60ml) best-quality gin from the freezer (or vodka, if you really insist)

Splash of dry vermouth, such as Noilly Prat

Lemon or olives, to garnish

A well-made martini is about preparation, speed, and style.

Pre-chill a 5oz (150ml) martini glass, either in the freezer or by filling with ice and water, then discarding. Splash a little vermouth into the glass, and discard any excess. Take the gin directly from the freezer, and pour a generous measure—aim for around 2oz/4 tbsp (60ml).

If using lemon to garnish, slice off a slim piece of zest. Bend this in two over the top of the drink (pith side facing you, so the oil sprays onto the drink's surface), then drop the zest into the glass and serve immediately. Alternatively, select a couple of plump olives—the fat green ones from Puglia are best—and spear on a toothpick. Drop them into the drink and serve. If this is too strong for you, add more vermouth, or shake the gin with ice to dilute it a little.

DAIQUIRI

This beautifully balanced cocktail (sweet, sour, and potent) emerged from Cuba at the end of the nineteenth century. It was born out of the local mixture of rum and limes, and served by an engineer, Jennings Cox, to his guests when they ran out of rum. In 1948, the recipe was set down by David Embury, and his ideal ratio of 8:2:1 (rum:lime:sugar) is yet to be bettered.

INGREDIENTS

2oz/4 tbsp (60ml) top-quality white rum, such as Brugal, Banks, or Bacardi Superior

1½ tbsp (25ml) freshly squeezed lime juice

1 tbsp (15ml) sugar syrup (either buy Monin or make your own with 1:1 water to sugar, heated together)

Ice cubes

Lime, to garnish

Chill a 5oz (150ml) martini glass, and fill a Boston shaker with wet ice cubes—in this drink, you need a little dilution. Pour in the rum, juice, and sugar syrup, and fit the glass top. Give it a rhythmic shake (the ice should shoot the whole length of the shaker) until condensation forms on the outside of the tin. Remove the glass, and fit the Hawthorne strainer over the tin beaker. Strain the daiquiri into the martini glass to remove any ice chips. Garnish with a swipe of lime around the rim of the glass, and—if you're feeling fancy— a strip of zest.

OLD FASHIONED

A real bartender's drink, this one, although because it's so time-consuming to make, few will thank you for ordering one. Its origins lie in Bourbon's heartland in Kentucky, at the Pendennis Club, where, according to cocktail lore, it was conceived around 1895.

INGREDIENTS

2oz/4 tbsp (60ml) bourbon

2 bar spoons brown sugar

2–3 dashes Angostura bitters

Ice cubes

Orange peel, to garnish

This drink takes its own sweet time to build, so be patient. Put about ¾oz/1½ tbsp (20ml) of bourbon, the sugar, and the bitters in an empty rocks glass and mix using the flat part of the bar spoon until the sugar is dissolved. Add just one cube of fresh ice and stir for a minute—this begins the dilution needed for the drink to taste perfect. Add ¾oz/1½ tbsp (20ml) more bourbon and another ice cube, and keep stirring for a couple more minutes. Add the final ¾oz/1½ tbsp (20ml) of bourbon and another two ice cubes, and keep stirring for a final two minutes. The drink should now be perfectly cold and mixed.

To garnish, go for a generous twist of orange zest (steer clear of the American penchant for maraschino cherries unless you are very sweet-toothed). Before you drop the zest into the drink, use it to spray a little orange oil over the surface for an extra-enticing smell. Savor and enjoy.

CHAPTER 6

COCKTAIL JOINTS

job they do, a good bartender will be only too delighted to demonstrate their insanely detailed knowledge. The more interested you are, the more they will be.

The other tactic is, having looked at the drinks list, to confidently order off-piste. Asking for a martinez, for example, is shorthand for saying, "I know what I'm doing here. Do you?" This little-known drink (at least, little-known outside the realms of alcohol geeks) is thought to be the forerunner to the martini—and, yeah, that does make it cool. Originally, it was made with genever (the precursor to gin, which is more often used nowadays), vermouth, and some maraschino liqueur. You have to like your liquor to enjoy this one—but that's just the point. Alternatively, call the shots with your own twist on a classic: an old fashioned is a great drink and will garner a certain amount of kudos, but what about one made with aged tequila rather than bourbon? It's a great variation that will certainly get the bartender thinking about what to serve you next.

A couple of well-placed questions will help you to establish a good rapport with your barman and ensure the drinks keep flowing.

AVOIDING THE TURKEYS

However many umbrellas there are in the glass, a bad drink will still be a bad drink. In fact, as a general rule, the more distractions there are decking out a cocktail, the worse it is likely to be. To ensure you always order the right drink for your mood, you need to get to know what "family" of cocktails you most enjoy. Since the end of the eighteenth century, a cocktail has been defined as a drink that combines a spirit with something sweet and something sour or bitter. In those days, they were thought to be good for you. Now we know that they just make you feel good. "A cock tail, then," an editor of an American newspaper wrote in 1806, "is a stimulating liquor composed of spirits of any kind, sugar, water, and bitters. It is vulgarly called a bittered sling."

CATEGORIZING COCKTAILS

In 1876, an American bartender called Jerry Thomas wrote a book called *How to Mix Drinks* or *The Bon-Vivant's Companion*, in which he cataloged the different kinds of mixed drink. Many of his categories are still used, more have been added, and more still have blurred the slippery definitions. However, a rough outline of what to expect if someone asks you whether to flip or sling is as follows.

Slings

Slings were the original cocktail: alcohol modified with something sweet and something bitter to create a mixed drink. They still (just about) exist today, most famously in the Singapore Sling, a gin and pineapple confection created in the legendary Raffles Hotel in Singapore. The sling's journey from its humble roots has not always been a happy one, and they are often best avoided.

Sours and Shorts

Sours and shorts are those drinks served in squat rocks glasses, and are invariably rather good. They major on liquor without getting too bogged down in the detail of a mixer, using instead citrus juice, occasionally a splash of egg white (see also Flips), which, like mustard in a salad dressing, works as an emulsifier, and something sweet. Famous examples are the whisky sour and the sidecar. A safe bet if you like drinks that get straight to the point.

Flips

Flips were originally a potent seafaring concoction of rum, beer, and sugar into which a scalding iron was dipped to make it foam. Over time, the hot-iron treatment has been replaced with the use of egg white, to create a similarly frothy drink but with less call for a forge in the bar. Flips based on dark spirits are most common, and these drinks make an excellent rich, winter evening cocktail. They can be sweet, but also extremely smooth and warming. Don't be afraid of the raw egg element either—it imparts no taste but gives a wonderfully smooth texture to your drink.

Cobblers

Cobblers were originally wine- or sherry-based drinks, built over lots and lots of ice (the cobbles, as some would have it) and garnished with plenty of fruit. The sherry version was hugely popular in the first half of the nineteenth century. If you see one on a cocktail list, it's worth investigating.

Long drinks

Long drinks are usually named after the glass they're served in: highballs. Highball cocktails are pretty uncomplicated— think gin & tonic or Cuba libre (rum & Coke)—and are perfect when you need a thirst-slaking refresher. Highballs made with juice rather than soda (with the exception of the bloody Mary) tend to be sweeter and heavier-going (like a sex on the beach) and are at the less sophisticated end of the spectrum.

Hot drinks

Hot drinks still have their place in the bar, most usually in the form of toddies, where hot water is added to a spirit—the traditional Scottish version would be honey, whisky, hot water, and cloves. While these may not actually be medically proven to cure colds, they certainly feel as though they might. This is a drink to order when you need to be warmed from the inside out.

Collins

The Collins family is also made up of long drinks—basically, your chosen spirit mixed with lemon juice, sugar, and water (or lemonade, as it's otherwise known). Made well, these are balanced and easy to drink. The fizz is Collins' bubblier younger sibling. It's served in a short glass, and made with carbonated soda water.

Champagne cocktails

Champagne cocktails, a sophisticated little clutch of drinks, are an interesting way to pep up a glass of the French fizz. The original and best, simply called the Champagne cocktail, is made with a sugar cube, a few drops of Angostura bitters, and a measure of Cognac. Look out for the French 75—a tempting variation using gin instead of Cognac, and lemon for the bitter element. Delicious.

Punches

Perhaps the liquid equivalent of a "sharing platter," punches are back in vogue with a vengeance. In Victorian times, punches usually began with a mulled, spiced wine, but nowadays they can be based on any cocktail made in batches. It's a great way to order drinks for parties, as there's no waiting for the next one to be mixed.

Shrubs

A genre of cocktail creeping back onto the most fashionable menus is the shrub. But be careful: the contents of your glass will vary depending on which side of the Atlantic you're on. In the UK, shrubs are based on alcoholic fruit syrups (usually from ancient medicinal recipes), whereas in the US, they are infused vinegar confections. These were developed to provide acidity in drinks when citrus was out of season, so fruit juice and spices are combined with drinking vinegar before being mixed into your spirit. If they're on the menu, this would be a great place to start drinking.

Classics

This category-crossing selection is made up of the drinks that bartenders favor. Order these with impunity, as every one of these cocktails is a credit to good taste. Usually, they will be grouped together on the menu, but if they don't appear, just ask. Any bartender worth his salt would be delighted to mix you one of the following:

Martinez: The precursor to the martini and made with genever rather than gin, which was yet to be imported into the US. The history of the martinez makes this a popular choice for many cocktail connoisseurs.

Punches are a good choice for parties, as long
as your guests don't overindulge.

Martini: Arguably the most famous of all the classics, a true
martini should be made with gin and vermouth, but many
would argue vodka is a perfectly acceptable substitute.

Classic daiquiri: A favorite of both Ernest Hemingway
and John F Kennedy, the daiquiri grew in popularity during
the 1940s when rationing meant whiskey and vodka
became increasingly hard to get hold of. The proximity of
America to Cuba meant rum could be procured relatively
easily and US drinkers quickly developed a taste for the
bitter sweet cocktail.

Sazerac: One of the first drinks made of whiskey, bitters, sugar, and absinthe, the Sazerac is regarded by many to be the first American cocktail.

Negroni: Currently enjoying something of a renaissance and cropping up on an increasing number of cocktail menus, this short, bitter, and super-cool aperitif is made with gin, vermouth, and Campari.

Old fashioned: This mix of bourbon, sugar, and bitters was originally created to balance some of the harshness of the whiskey. It's also a drink that encourages experimentation and bartenders will all have their own unique take on it.

Sidecar: Made with Cognac, Cointreau, and lemon juice, the Sidecar is shortly approaching its 100th birthday.

Manhattan: Originally made with rye whiskey, vermouth, and bitters, this cocktail dates back to the 1870s. Contemporary versions often contain bourbon rather than rye and are garnished with a cherry.

Clover club: A pre-Prohibition drink that's a mixture of lemon juice, gin, and grenadine, this cocktail is named after an exclusive Philadelphia men's club frequented by various industry tycoons.

The above selection is a non-exhaustive list, and there is a case to argue for the inclusion of many more excellent cocktails. But before long, you'll have your own list of favorites.

CHAPTER 7

PUBS AND BARS: AN EVOLUTION

The locals were pleased to see David Beckham had decided to turn his back on retirement.

The craft masters

Identifying marks: Staffed by chaps who look like the bearded members of Mumford & Sons (lumberjack shirts, skinny jeans, and cool tattoos), craft-beer establishments are most commonly identified by a scruffy-but-scrubbed-up feel, with chalkboards enthusiastically promoting a changing host of unusual beers, often dominated by IPAs. Expect bar snacks of the man-food variety, which often appear in place of a fully fledged menu. After all, the emphasis here is on beer.

Patterns of behavior: The modern-day craft-beer enthusiasts are not the geeks of old, and are masters of a gentle, disheveled kind of cool. They tend to travel in small packs and won't be averse to being approached if you wish to seek an opinion or a recommendation.

How to handle an encounter: Prepare yourself for much talk of hops. Perhaps even cite a favorite: "Personally, I don't think you can beat Fuggles," etc., and you'll want to be familiar with the craft-beer basics (see chapter 3). Ask for what's in that's new, what the bartender suggests, and ask to try before you buy—tasters will be readily handed out. It's also worth remembering that real ale is a live product, meaning that it's still fermenting in the cask, so it is prone to problems. A good establishment will spot a bad pint, but always keep your eye open for funky smells or unexpectedly cloudy liquid. The staff here will be experts in their field and should be treated as such. Do not ask for an alcopop or, worse still, a pint of Coors.

The brewpub

Identifying marks: Easily identified by the fact that it, well, contains a brewery, the most attractive parts of which are likely to be visible. Food will be of little or no consequence, although occasionally you may find snacks, which are aimed as pairings with the beers on offer.

Patterns of behavior: Although they share much common ground with craft-beer venues, brewpubs have taken their enthusiasm for beer one step further. On-site brewing facilities mean that customers will range from a devoted tribe of ale aficionados to, more commonly, beer tourists who come for the experience. You're more likely to come across a brewpub in the US or Canada, where the craft-beer movement has more traction and the large breweries have less of a stranglehold.

How to handle an encounter: Often, licensing laws in brewpubs mean that you'll be limited in the amount of beer you can purchase (expect the equivalent of one pint), so be selective in your choices. Try not to be swayed by novelty: beers themed around an event or a season are unlikely to taste better than the core range. And, obviously, only attempt to order beer brewed on the premises; other requests may cause offence. Constructive criticism or feedback will be welcomed.

The rural idyll
Identifying marks: A distinctly British breed. Sited in a quaint spot with more than a whiff of Merrie Olde England about it, these history-imbued buildings have been the meeting point of communities for generations. Damp dogs and Wellington boots litter the door's well-worn sill, while an array of stuffed creatures, horse brasses, and blazing open fires fill the black-beamed interior.

Patterns of behavior: Patrons will typically include a few gently murmuring folk who've sat in the same spot at the bar, drinking from the same tankard, for decades; a smattering of genuine locals who are in to shoot the breeze over a quiet drink; and, come Sunday lunchtime, a crew of wax-jacketed, Labrador-wielding weekenders, exclaiming about how cheap it is compared to London.

How to handle an encounter: Do not excite or antagonize locals—you are on their turf. A curt nod is more appropriate than the trumpeting cry of "gin & tonics all round!" Equally, consider this fair warning: if you pull up a barstool next to a local, you are likely to be on the receiving end of the same tales he's been trotting out for forty years, and may have difficulty extricating yourself. Assuming the pub has plenty of custom, this will be one of the best places in the world to try properly kept real ale—a seasoned landlord and a good cellar mean that your pint will be an excellent one. Beware, though, the tumbleweed tavern. For beer to be in peak condition, it needs to be used quickly. Plenty of orders mean that the beer is pulled through the lines regularly, casks are finished fast, and the beer you'll be drinking will be in the best possible condition.

The genuine gastro-pub

Identifying marks: Provenance, provenance, provenance: everything from the salted nuts to the fruit juice to the bar staff will have been meticulously sourced. Although this may have the appearance of a pub, you are about to experience restaurant-grade, artfully casual food, choosing from a menu that features parts of the animal you may never wish to consume (chitterling pie, anyone?). Nose-to-tail eating is the name of the game.

Patterns of behavior: Foodies will roam their territory with a hawkish eye searching out anyone who may be ordering more adventurously (this is the most middle-class form of competitive eating). Look out for food bloggers sporting their Nikon D7000 and industriously taking snaps of anything that's about to pass their lips.

How to handle an encounter: With enthusiasm. Any interest shown will be rewarded with more engaged service and the opportunity, perhaps, to sample off-menu or unusual items. Don't miss the chance to try well-crafted beers alongside your gastro food. Chances are you'll be faced with an appetizing selection to rival anything you'd get in a top restaurant. Experiment with different combinations, but, generally speaking, think of ale as the red wine (nuttier, richer) and lager as the white wine (lighter, more floral). If you need a pairing that's got lots of acidity (where you might have a sauvignon blanc wine, for example), then try an intensely hoppy IPA for an equally palate-tingling result. And don't forget the sweet stuff. Porter and stout are stunning with chocolate, so there's no need to skip dessert. Beware of gastro-pub imitations—you don't want to pay over the odds for the equivalent of souped-up TV dinners (ready meals).

"I read on Twitter that the food here's almost as good as the photo opportunities."

The dive bar

Identifying marks: Broken jukebox, sticky tables, bowls of stale nuts, pool tables, an uninspiring selection of drinks on offer (whatever you do, don't ask for a cocktail here), a distinctive smell of disinfectant laced with a soupçon of urinal are all key characteristics. Expect also Thursday-night quizzes and Friday-night karaoke—the owner's best effort at luring in the punters.

Patterns of behavior: Although, at first glance, this genre of pub may have little to commend it, there may well be a die-hard pack of locals who disagree with your initial assessment and for whom this is an extension of their living room. They will treat "their" pub—and anyone unwelcome who comes into it—exactly as they please, and protect it fiercely and vociferously.

How to handle an encounter: Voice extreme opinions with extreme care. Don't stare or linger. Don't jump the line for the pool table. Don't knock anyone's drink and don't let your guard down.

The European dive bar

Identifying marks: A common venue in northern European countries such as Denmark, Germany, and Poland, the bar's ear-bleedingly loud music will announce that you've found the spot long before you see it. Whether the venue is cavernous or tiny, you should expect low-level lighting, eye-watering quantities of ban-flouting cigarette smoke, decent booze, free-flowing shots of local spirits, and—if you're lucky—really good sausage on the side.

Patterns of behavior: Social groupings generally blend into one, with a uniform verging on Goth being standard issue. Female attendance can sometimes be low; often it is male-dominated, heavy-booted groups that tend to form the bulk of the crowd.

How to handle an encounter: Although the clientele may look a little intimidating to the casual observer, don't be put off. Out-of-towners are usually regarded with friendly interest, especially if you're fluent in enough music genres to fuel conversation. Continental-strength beer (look out for the number of Xs on the pump clip) served in liters should help you overcome any shyness by the time you have reached the bottom of your first glass. If all your initial attempts at engaging the locals fail, try talking about that great leveler—football.

The Irish pub
Identifying marks: Known the world over—from Tipperary to Tokyo—and heralded by names such as O'Brien's, O'Neil's, Flanagan's, Fitzgerald's, or Murphy's, Irish pubs are easily singled out by the green-and-gold Celtic font used on all merchandizing and signage, the prevalence of impressive collections of Guinness advertising, and the often mystifying screenings of Six Nations rugby and GAA games, such as hurling and Gaelic football.

. . . .

No matter where you are on the planet, you're never more than an hour's drive away from the nearest Irish pub.

Patterns of behavior: Everyone here, regardless of what their birth certificate might imply, is Irish. Whether you're in Texas or Tipperary, are local, or just passing through, discussions of lineage are par for the course. Irish bars attract all sorts, drawn in by the universal hospitality. Backpackers, old-timers, business executives—you never know whom you might meet.

How to handle an encounter: Order as much Guinness and Irish whiskey as you can stomach, while making new best friends and talking freely to anyone within earshot. Revel in the lack of boundaries, animosity, or cultural divide as you are united in your common Irish roots. Especially to be commended on St. Patrick's Day, when full-scale inebriation is considered mandatory. People often spuriously claim that Guinness tastes better in Ireland than anywhere else, but it's the same barrels being served in Dublin as in Denver. The only likely difference is that one barrel is fresh, while the other might be left to linger (and even Guinness can only wait for so long).

CHAPTER 8

ALL-DAY DRINKING: A SURVIVAL GUIDE

Weddings, summer barbeques, corporate days out, company Christmas parties... occasions sometimes arise that require stout drinking bouts. The key to navigating such an event is to begin with a strategy, and stick to it.

THE 10 COMMANDMENTS

Here are the rules for all-day drinking. Choose to ignore them at your peril.

1 Thou shalt not drink on an empty stomach

You know this already. It doesn't matter if you think a pre-arrival snack will have an adverse effect on your silhouette, or if you claim to have only a half-eaten jar of pickles in the fridge: you must start the day with a decent, stomach-lining meal. Getting drunk is simply a case of you imbibing alcohol faster than your body can process it. If you down a glass of wine without having eaten any food, it will be absorbed straight into your bloodstream and have an almost instant effect. However, with a bacon sandwich in your stomach, that process will be slowed, allowing you to be more in control of how you are being affected by your drinks. So go eat.

2 Thou shalt know thy limits

Male, female, fat, thin, muscly, scrawny—there are countless physical factors that affect what that pint of Stella Artois or glass of Champagne will do to you. Women have less water and more body-fat than men and so don't hold their drink as well. Equally, the smaller your build, the less tolerance you will have. Some ethnic groups can process alcohol better than others. Europeans, with their agricultural background and historic exposure to grain alcohol, for example, have higher levels of enzymes that break down booze than do Australian Aborigines. So be realistic about what your body is capable of if you really want to avoid any embarrassing situations as the day progresses. And don't feel like you have to match your 18-stone, body-builder friend drink for drink— it will only end in tears.

3 Thou shalt not forget to drink water

If you're dehydrated, the alcohol in your drink will be absorbed at a higher concentration than if you manage to down the odd bottle of Evian. It's dehydration, too, that leads to the most horrible hangover symptoms the following day. The most strategic way to try to keep your water levels appropriately topped up is to have one glass of water for every alcoholic drink. Just make sure you've scoped out where the bathrooms are.

4 Thou shalt avoid carbonation

You've heard people say that Champagne goes straight to their head? Chances are they're feeling its effects because of the fizz. Any carbonated or sparkling drink is absorbed faster than a still one because the extra pressure created by the gas forces the alcohol into the bloodstream. So, for all-day drinking etiquette, this means limiting the amount of carbonated drinks to a minimum, to help steady the pace at which alcohol gets into your system.

"What's the Russian for '*save me a vol-au-vent*'?"

5 Thou shalt stalk the canapé tray

In Russia, where drinking is practically a national sport, shots of vodka are most usually consumed alongside tasty morsels of, say, smoked fish or pickles (apparently, the acid and brine neutralize alcohol, although there's little proof of this). Ensure you do the same and make friends with whoever is circulating the canapé tray. If you have one snack alongside every drink—by the way, there's no need to choose neat vodka—then you'll go some way to slowing down the absorption of alcohol.

6 Thou shalt choose thy poison with care

Take it slow, take it steady—and make careful choices when ordering your drinks. If you're going for beer, choose "cooking strength" lagers rather than craft or Continental brews that pack a heftier percentage of alcohol. For wine, avoid alcohol-packed Aussie Shiraz and go instead for a lighter Beaujolais (you've probably just saved about 4 per cent ABV), and if you're drinking white, opt for a Riesling or a Prosecco (go easy—see commandment 4), which tend to have a lower ABV. Order singles, rather than doubles, when drinking spirits. If your wine is being topped up by a circulating waitress, finish each glass before accepting a refill, so you can keep track of how much you've had. Avoid anything that's labeled export strength and—it goes without saying— steer clear of high-strength liquor such as overproof rum or absinthe. At 68 per cent ABV, absinthe does not make the heart grow fonder.

7 Thou shalt not do shots

No matter how funny it seemed at the time, you do not want your boss reminding you about the incident with the Jägerbombs (and the hilarious song you made up about him) the next day.

8 Thou shalt avoid using caffeine as a pick-me-up

Adding caffeine to an alcoholic mix can make you feel like a superhero, but if you're turning to coffee thinking it will help you power on through another few drinks, then chances are you've already had enough. Using espresso to self-medicate can increase your metabolism and may actually boost the rate at which liquor is absorbed by your body. That's probably not the result you were hoping for.

Knowing when to call it a night is key to being a successful drinker.

9 Thou shalt keep a cab number handy

Planning your exit is a crucial part of your drinking strategy. If you can do it without appearing rude, you may wish to make a very discreet exit. Sneaking off will mean you avoid any peer-pressure moments of "Noooo, stay for one more," and if everyone is well oiled, they are unlikely to be keeping track of what time you left anyway. Thank your host, call a cab, and take your dignity home with you.

10 Thou shalt hope for the best but prepare for the worst

Before bed, drink a large glass of water. All of it. If you've been dancing or out in the sun, then opt for a rehydration sachet to replace lost salts. And now is the time for a pre-emptive painkiller if you suspect you're going to need it.

CHAPTER 9

BLOWING THE BUDGET (AND KEEPING YOUR COOL)

THE RIGHT WAY

THE WRONG WAY

Here's a true story. A man walks into a bar—let's call it the Loft, in Luton. He's had a bit of Dutch courage already, and he approaches two girls who are deep in conversation over a couple of cosmopolitans.

HOW NOT TO LOOK COOL

Man: Hey, girls, how you doin'?

Girls: [sigh] We're fine, thanks—just, you know—trying to catch up.

Man: [undeterred] Can I buy you a drink?

Girls: No, thanks, we're fine.

Man: [still undeterred, reaching for pocket] Are you sure? I can show you my bank balance?

Girls: [horrified] No! That really won't be necessary.

The man persists, the bank advice slip remains folded, until eventually...

Girls: Oh, go on, we'll have a drink. Get us something lovely and bubbly.

The man disappears, gleefully, to the bar, only to return some time later clutching two warm Bacardi Breezers. The girls exit stage left.

The moral of the tale relates to taste and money—notoriously difficult bedfellows. It isn't just the Jersey Shore cast member or the sports star who can suffer something of an etiquette malfunction as soon as there is a little cash in their pocket. It can happen anywhere on the financial food chain. Our Luton man, gauche enough to want to demonstrate proof of earnings, was at least being upfront about the fact he thought that being in the black might be just the bait to catch a girl. (He was pitching the wrong deal to the wrong duo: these dames were expecting a demonstration of his good taste, which, to be clear, didn't involve alcopops.)

So, if you do really want to treat yourself and throw some cash at a night out (or in), how do you do it and remain on the right side of cool? The first thing to point out is that wealth is relative: the chap next to you at the bar in Manhattan or Mayfair might be as rich as Croesus, but you'd never know it because of the inconspicuous way he consumes. Equally, the group dancing on the tables amid a sea of Grey Goose magnums and sparklers may have just burned all they (or their parents) have earned in a peacocking display that is going to make the morning hangover the most painful yet.

One of the more eye-watering bar bills in recent times was run up by a

20-something financier in a club in Liverpool, England. Included in the £203,948 (over $300,000) total was a 30-liter bottle of Armand de Brignac Champagne (which redefines flash), and an almost £20K ($30K) service charge (which isn't far off the average UK salary). It's the kind of extreme decadence that leaves a bad taste in your mouth.

GO BIG OR GO HOME

The smartest way to splurge your cash, as a generalization, is to avoid anything that comes with a "world's largest" label. Unless you are in it just for show—in which case, go ahead—then you are being duped by the group of marketeers who sat around wondering how to appeal to the most conspicuous consumer. Some brands have been engineered to appeal to just the kind of customer who buys according to the heft of a price tag, rather than according to what's in the bottle. Vodka, for example, is never going to taste any better because you are drinking it from a magnum (the equivalent of two 75cl bottles), rather than a conventional bottle. The contents are identical, and the only thing you are paying a premium for is the amount that the extra volume might impress your neighbors.

Size matters

In the world of wine, however, bottle size does matter. Experts agree that larger formats have a positive influence on taste, as fine wines actually age better in them. The liquid is thought to mature at a slower rate, to develop finer nuances of flavor, and to be of a more consistent quality than the standard-size bottle, thanks to the smaller air-to-liquid ratio between wine and cork. Although there are lots of large-format bottles available, the magnum is considered to be the optimum environment for aging wine, so expect to pay more than double the price of two 75cl bottles. It should be worth the outlay. However, a word of caution with regard to Champagne: it is extremely rare for the French fizz to be aged in anything larger than a magnum. If you're buying yourself a Methuselah (eight bottles), a Balthazar (16 bottles), or a Nebuchadnezzar (20 bottles), it will have been filled just before shipping, and so will offer no improvement in wine quality compared to a standard size. Once again, all your cash is buying is cachet.

If you really want to spend big, then ignore the sparkler-clad attractions of the super-sized super-brands and concentrate instead on age and rarity. There is something totally unique about drinking a piece of liquid history that will never be repeated: a wine, brandy, or Scotch that was made by artisans who couldn't begin to imagine the world where their product would be consumed. Early in 2013, a bottle of brandy, Croizet Cognac Leonie 1858, was purchased for $156,760—the highest price ever paid for a Cognac. Was it

worth it? That's up for debate, but one thing's for certain. At more than 150 years old, it would be impossible to taste anything equivalent to this exact bottle anywhere else in the world. Our flash young Liverpool-based trader spent more than this on a single bottle of bubbles from Armand de Brignac, a brand first featured in Jay-Z's "Show Me What You've Got" video, and which was only established in 2006. (Fittingly, Armand de Brignac call this bottle "Midas.")

It's not just spirits that can showcase something old and unique—look at the wine list for really unusual bottles. Often the oldest and rarest bottles on a list are sold to the consumer without a huge margin because of the prestige garnered by carrying such exclusive stock. While the standard restaurant markup is three times the wholesale price, in almost all topnotch establishments the markup decreases as the wholesale cost increases. This means that a really expensive bottle may only carry a 50 per cent markup. Yes, this does mean that the 1969 Hermitage is arguably good value, so go ahead.

HOW TO DRINK LIKE AN OLIGARCH (EVEN IF YOU'RE NOT)

We can't all afford to swill Château Petrus like it's going out of fashion, but there is a brilliantly democratic new way to drink wine. In recent years, an excellent innovation, the Enomatic wine dispenser, has been popping up in wine bars. It allows an establishment to open any bottle—no matter how delicate or how old—and sell it by the glass, while preserving the integrity of the remaining wine for at least three weeks. (An inert gas is introduced into the bottle, meaning that the wine can't oxidize.) While wines by the glass are usually a

So, Oleg, if we're going to make it back to shore in time for happy hour and karaoke at the bar, we'd better get moving.

ferociously uneconomical way to buy—the first glass usually covers the restaurant's cost for the rest of the bottle—bars with Enomatic dispensers allow the consumer to try wines at a fair price without risk of wasting the rest of the bottle. For example, at one such bar in London, The Kensington Wine Rooms, you can try a glass of Pomerol (a bottle usually sells for around £80-plus/$123) for just over £10 ($15). The dispenser is an excellent way to investigate fine wine without having to pay a premium. Now that's worth raising a glass to.

INDEX